Original title:
Breeze Through the Palms

Copyright © 2025 Creative Arts Management OÜ
All rights reserved.

Author: George Mercer
ISBN HARDBACK: 978-1-80581-541-9
ISBN PAPERBACK: 978-1-80581-068-1
ISBN EBOOK: 978-1-80581-541-9

Caressing Wind and Verdant Dreams

In the jungle gym of foliage,
Monkeys swing with sheer delight,
Leaves tickle faces, oh what fun,
As squirrels join the wild flight.

A toucan scores with goofy calls,
While lizards dance on branches high,
Nature's laughter fills the air,
Underneath a sunny sky.

Nature's Gentle Murmur

What's that noise? Oh, just a leaf,
Whispering secrets, oh so sly,
With a rustle and a giggle,
Who knew trees could make you cry?

The owl hoots a fumbled joke,
While crickets chirp their own refrain,
Nature's chat is full of gags,
Sometimes a little bit insane.

Fronds in the Evening Glow

Dancing shadows on the ground,
As the sun yawns, stretching slow,
Fronds wave to the moon's sweet grin,
Evening chatter steals the show.

Fireflies tease with flickering lights,
In a waltz that's quite absurd,
Leaves roll their eyes at the scene,
They've got the funniest word.

A Tryst with Nature's Breath

A giggling stream makes silly sounds,
Bouncing over rocks, it flows,
Fish flip their tails with joy and flair,
As turtles strike a pose, who knows?

The flowers lean in for a chuckle,
While bees buzz past in wild haste,
Nature's this grand comedic act,
In every nook, it's a great taste.

Tropical Dreams Under Canopies

In the shade where critters peek,
A coconut drops with a party squeak,
Laughter echoes, we can't ignore,
As lizards dance and crabs explore.

Mangoes fall with a juicy plop,
While parrots squawk and never stop,
Sun hats fly with a gusty cheer,
While we dodge the bees that buzz too near.

The Sound of Leaves in Play

Whispers of green, a leafy shout,
As squirrels chatter, there's no doubt,
Branches swing with a playful twist,
Inviting secrets not to be missed.

Bamboo shoots like a drum that beat,
While ants march in a funny fleet,
Petals swirl like a confetti cloud,
Making the shyest flowers proud.

Melodies of the Ocean's Kiss

Waves clap hands on a sandy shore,
Seagulls croon a cheeky encore,
Shells rattle like they're in a band,
While jellyfish do the tango on the sand.

A crab moonwalks in clumsy style,
Sincerely adding to the nautical file,
With every splash, a giggling cheer,
As ocean tunes soothe all our fears.

Where Leaves and Sky Converge

When sunlight winks through leafy gates,
And a breeze teases the playful plates,
The sky wears clouds like a silly hat,
As owls snicker at the jolly chat.

In crooked nests, the young ones jest,
Chasing shadows, what a quest!
High above, the laughter swells,
Where nature sings its silly bells.

Echoes of Nature's Embrace

The trees dance wildly, what a sight,
Their branches wiggle, oh what a fright!
A parrot squawks with such glee,
Chasing off the squirrel's cup of tea.

Laughter spills like morning dew,
As leaves whisper secrets, just us two.
A funky monkey swings above,
Singing to the rhythm of a tree trunk love.

Secrets of the Swaying Canopies

With every gust, the leaves conspire,
They gossip gladly, oh how they tire!
A lizard sunbathes, acting cool,
While ants march by, they rule the pool.

Napping turtles share wild tales,
Of wiggly worms in glittering trails.
A gecko dances, what a show,
His moves are slick, we all yell, "Whoa!"

Serenity in the Shade

Under the shade, we find our fun,
A picnic spread, with goodies to shun.
The sandwich flies, a daring leap,
While fruit rolls down in a merry sweep.

A passing breeze makes the napkins fly,
Oh no, not the chips, don't let them lie!
Laughter cascades like melting ice,
In the shade, everything feels so nice.

Melody of the Gentle Wind

A ticklish wind whispers my name,
It teases the flowers, what a game!
Each blossom giggles, sways to the tune,
Under the sun, like a silly cartoon.

The clouds join in, a fluffy parade,
Creating shadows, a woodland charade.
With a whoosh and a hum, they play along,
Nature's chorus, a funny song.

Warm Embrace of the Tropics

The sun's a prankster, bright and bold,
It tickles your skin, like stories told.
Coconuts giggle, while monkeys laugh,
Sunbathing crabs take a sunlit bath.

Lizards dance on branches, a quirky sight,
While jellybeans float in tropical night.
A parrot squawks jokes, oh what a fuss,
As warm air wraps you like a friendly bus.

Flickering Light Through Leaves

Shadows play tag in the canopy high,
While fireflies waltz, a flamboyant sky.
Mangoes dangle, ripe jokes in the air,
A gecko narrates, with tales beyond compare.

The rustling palms whisper cheeky remarks,
While squirrels juggle snacks, hitting their marks.
In the golden glow, laughter unfolds,
As sunlight tumbles and giggles untold.

Essence of the Hidden Grove

The hidden grove buzzes with mischief and cheer,
Where fruit flies rap and the parrots jeer.
Tropical scents tickle your nose,
While frogs croak riddles that nobody knows.

Vines play tug-of-war, giggling around,
With a playful breeze, they spin in the sound.
Bamboo rustles, gossiping leaves,
In this quirky realm, humor weaves.

Tales of Tropic Serenity

Tropic tales unfold with a chuckle and cheer,
As waves crash and whisper secrets to hear.
Laughter spills over from cascades above,
While starfruit smiles, glowing with love.

The sea winks knowingly, a cheeky tease,
As seagulls perform acrobatics with ease.
In this land of giggles and sunburnt dreams,
Every moment bursts with light-hearted themes.

Nature's Silent Dance

The trees sway side to side, quite spry,
Like dancers in a dream that's sky-high.
A squirrel twirls, thinking he's hot stuff,
But trips on a nut—oh, wasn't that tough!

The grass tickles toes, in fits and giggles,
While birds debate how best to do wiggles.
A rabbit hops in a cape made of fluff,
All join the fun, but no one is tough!

Twilight Hues in the Breeze

As day melts into shades of tangerine,
The lizards strike poses, quite the keen scene.
They flash little smiles, as if to say,
"Catch us if you can, we'll make you play!"

The dusky air ginormously grins,
While crickets compose their quirky spin wins.
Fireflies flicker like tiny lamps turned on,
Their waltzing so wild, you'd think they were drawn!

Lush Horizons Unfolding

The hills roll like dough, all soft and round,
As goats do karate, they twirl and bound.
"Keep your feet on the ground!" cries a wise old tree,
But the goats just laugh, "That's too boring for me!"

Mosses chat secrets and gossip the day,
While mushrooms wear hats—what a fancy display!
"Who wore it best?" they casually discuss,
But all are just winners—no need to fuss!

Petals of Light Amongst Leaves

Sunlight splashes colors, a painter at work,
While butterflies prance—oh, what a perk!
They flutter their wings, putting on a show,
"Hey, flower, can you do that?" but none can glow!

Petals peel off like stickers in rages,
Dancing in circles, becoming bright pages.
Laughing upturned, the blooms share a joke,
As bees join in, buzzing like a folk poke!

Tranquil Moments in the Shade

Under the umbrella of leafy green,
A squirrel rehearses for his acorn scene.
In sunlight he's free, in shadows he speaks,
A dance of his tail, with whimsical tweaks.

The mockingbird chirps a curious tune,
A raccoon chimes in, with a laugh and a swoon.
They share their tales of mischief and fun,
While winking at folks who forgot how to run.

Shimmering Leaves and Sky

Golden rays tickle the emerald bunch,
While butterflies flutter, a colorful lunch.
The leaves giggle gently, a playful delight,
As ants march in line, preparing for flight.

Clouds drift by, donning a silly old face,
The sun plays peek-a-boo, a lighthearted chase.
A bumblebee buzzes, "I'm late, can't you see?"
While a lizard rolls over, just sipping his tea.

Nature's Whispering Spirit

Whispers of green in a world full of cheer,
A frog croaks loudly, "Is anybody here?"
The flowers all chuckle, their petals so bright,
As ladybugs giggle in pure, sheer delight.

The whispers grow louder, a rumor of fun,
As a turtle gives high-fives to everyone.
The grass grows a bit, wearing dewdrop beads,
While ants plan a party, fulfilling their needs.

Enchanted Grove Element

In the heart of the grove, mischief takes flight,
With squirrels debating who's fastest at night.
Roots weave their tales as the shadows all dance,
And daisies join in with a spontaneous prance.

Owl on a branch, he hoots just for kicks,
Laughing at critters trying silly tricks.
Laughter resounds among branches and leaves,
As nature performs in a costume of peas.

Silhouettes of a Gentle Day

In the shade where shadows play,
I dance and bob, come what may.
Swaying tall, the monkeys cheer,
They want my hat, oh dear, oh dear!

Lizards race with wiggly tails,
While I chase ghosts of silly gales.
A parrot talks back with a squawk,
I'm convinced it's planning to mock.

The sunbeams giggle on my face,
I trip on roots, it's quite the race.
The trees chuckle as I fall,
Oh, what a clumsy, funny ball!

As night creeps in with a lollipop hue,
I swear the stars wink, just for you.
When the moon peeks in to say,
"Don't trip again, you'll be okay!"

Nature's Embrace in Stillness

Oh, look at that bird, what a sight!
He dances like it's Friday night.
A squirrel's got a nut on parade,
I wonder if he'll join the charade.

In the silence, a frog croaks loud,
Telling off a passing cloud.
A snail thinks he's a speedy chap,
But he sleeps and naps in a cozy lap.

Roaming where worries are lighter,
The ants debate who's the fighter.
"Let's rock, let's roll," they seem to say,
But always they wander the same old way.

The sun bows down, it's almost late,
I giggle at nature — isn't it great?
With a yawn, I nod at tomorrow's fun,
When all this nonsense has just begun!

Lullaby Beneath the Foliage

Under leaves, a song does hum,
A squirrel's dance, a comical thrum.
A parrot yells, 'Hey, look at me!'
While salsa-playing ants drink green tea.

Coconut trees sway with a grin,
As lizards race, their heads in spin.
The rustling sound is quite the tease,
It tickles your toes and makes you sneeze!

Caress of the Island Air

The fan's too lazy to give a blow,
While the sun takes a peek, just to show.
Sunglasses slide down my nose with glee,
As I trip on the sand—oh, woe is me!

The weekend's here; it's time to play,
But jellyfish want to join the fray!
With each step back—I dance with grace,
And wish I had brought my swimming space!

Shadows and Sunlight

Shadows leap like frogs in jest,
While sunlight plays a hidden quest.
A crab scuttles with an elegant flick,
And blinks at me, it's quite the trick!

Count the seams in the sky's decor,
As puffy clouds start their encore.
Laughter echoes, a bright new tune,
Even the sun joins in, so rude!

The Hushed Tides of Green

In the hush of green, a secret lurks,
A chubby iguana, it slyly smirks.
It steals the spotlight, legs so stout,
While I can only laugh and pout.

The waves bring ripples of mischief proud,
As children build castles, oh so loud!
Nearby, a toucan giggles in flight,
Painting sunsets with colors bright.

Flickers of Light Through Fronds

Sunlight giggles, plays along,
Leaves do sway, a leafy song.
A curious squirrel jumps with glee,
Chasing shadows, wild and free.

Palm trees chuckle, swaying low,
Tickling toes as breezes flow.
They whisper secrets, oh so sly,
"Don't look up, or you might cry!"

A hammock sings in sunlit grace,
Spinning tales of a sleepy face.
Coconuts grin, taking their time,
While seagulls circle, plotting mime.

The world's a circus, laughter loud,
Under foliage where dreams are bowed.
Nature claps, a show to see,
In the jungle, just you and me.

Soft Summer Secrets

In the shade where whispers dwell,
Sandals flip with a merry yell.
Among the palms, a dance unfolds,
As secrets spill from leaves like gold.

A lizard darts, a flash of green,
Catching rays while looking keen.
"Why so still?" I ask a frog,
"Just waiting for my morning jog!"

Coconut smiles, a fun-filled drink,
With every sip, I start to think.
The sun waves hello, a playful tease,
That tickles toes and stirs the breeze.

Underneath this leafy roof,
Every laugh becomes the proof.
Summer giggles, wonders play,
In this paradise, let's stay.

The Green Symphony

Leaves are drummers, tapping light,
Cacophony of colors, what a sight!
A parrot chirps a merry tune,
While swinging bees buzz a monsoon.

In the distance, a monkey swings,
Counting all the silly things.
A palm tree's hat is quite the name,
It sways and calls, "Join this game!"

Bamboo flutes serenade the sun,
As playful waves begin to run.
A crab gets ready for its dance,
"Hey there, fish, let's take a chance!"

Foliage rustles, whispers loud,
While the sun flips behind a cloud.
In this garden of joy and cheer,
Nature's music draws us near.

Nature's Gentle Caress

A gentle touch from leafy hands,
Caressing cheeks like magic strands.
Chirping crickets laugh with style,
While the sun beams in playful guile.

Palm leaves tease with a rustling laugh,
Telling tales of the day's half.
A butterfly flutters with grace and flair,
Sipping nectar without a care.

Turtles chuckle, slow yet wise,
"Life's a crawl, no need for ties."
The ocean winks, with foamy play,
Saying "Come join the fray today!"

Under this canopy, time stands still,
Every giggle here is a thrill.
Nature's touch, a sweet embrace,
Where laughter finds its rightful place.

Shadows at Sunset

Silly shadows dance and play,
Chasing crickets' notes away.
A coconut slips, oh what a sight,
Rolling down as if in flight.

Giggling leaves in evening's glow,
Whisper secrets we don't know.
A monkey swings with cheeky grin,
Stealing snacks, let the fun begin!

Palm trees sway in laughter's tune,
Underneath the watching moon.
A parrot complains about his luck,
Saying, 'I'd rather ride a truck!'

As shadows stretch and night draws near,
The island life gives a hearty cheer.
With every gust, we strike a pose,
In this game that nature chose.

Echoes Among the Fronds

Amidst the fronds, a ruckus starts,
With rustling leaves like secret arts.
A lizard slides on his quest for flies,
While crabs compete in clever disguise.

A toucan's laugh, so bright, so loud,
Makes even Hermit crabs feel proud.
Tickling palms with playful thrusts,
Noting who here truly trusts.

As sunlight dances, colors burst,
Chasing shadows, who's the first?
A squirrel with style, wearing a hat,
Proclaims, 'Nature's where it's at!'

Echoes call from leaf to leaf,
Filling hearts with joyful belief.
Each rustle a punchline to enjoy,
In this comedic tropical ploy.

The Gentle Song of the Shore

The ocean hums a silly tune,
As seagulls dance beneath the moon.
With every wave, a giggle froths,
Reminding us of playful oaths.

Sandcastles crumble with a splash,
Building kingdoms in a flash.
A crab in a hat struts with flair,
Claiming the castle for his lair!

With every shell, a story spins,
Of pirate ships and misplaced pins.
The tide tickles toes in retreat,
While laughter echoes, oh so sweet.

The gentle waves, a comedy show,
Whispering secrets only we know.
As the stars blink in evening gloom,
We share our jokes, our hearts, our room.

Swaying Elegance

Funky palms sway left and right,
In a dance that feels just right.
A toucan struts with style so grand,
Trying to impress a beach band.

The breeze teases with a playful twist,
While sea turtles join the list.
A surfboard lands with a clumsy thud,
Sending up a spray of sand and mud.

Sun hats fly like kites on high,
While fish below just swim on by.
A cat in shades is posing cool,
Claiming the beach like a furry fool.

In this elegance of fun and cheer,
Nature hosts a party here!
With laughter flowing, sand in tow,
We find a joy that steals the show.

Radiance in the Canopy

High above, the leaves do dance,
Swishing skirts in sunlit prance.
A coconut drops, a sudden thud,
Nature's marbles? No, just a dud!

Birds are chirping, making a scene,
Trying to sing, but it's all quite mean.
A parrot squawks a joke so grand,
Only to be met by a quiet strand.

The shadows shift, they start to play,
Hide-and-seek with the light of day.
Laughter floats on the gallant air,
As the palm fronds tease with flair.

Each gust tells tales, both ragged and fun,
With giggles and snickers from everyone.
Oh, the canopy's rapture, such a gay sight,
A comedy show, day turns to night!

The Poetry of Leaves

Oh, how they flutter, a leafy brigade,
Conspiring wildly in sun's warm shade.
Tickling the trunks with their witty ways,
Turning each moment to jovial plays.

Leaves flip through verses, oh what a rhyme,
Counting each rustle like passing time.
A frond gives a wink, while another high-fives,
In their leafy world, mirth truly thrives.

Sunbeams giggle, reflecting their glee,
As the leaves conspire, wild and free.
With shadows that dance much like a mime,
In the theatre of light, they share a good time!

So here's to the voices in green foliage,
Spread laughter like seeds through the leafy college.
For in this haven of humor and cheer,
Each leaf holds a story we'd love to hear!

Palm Leaves' Serenade

Hear the whispers among the green,
A song of laughter, a hilarious scene.
Palm leaves strum like a ticklish harp,
They shake with mirth, oh what a lark!

Gusts tease the branches, a playful blow,
Poking fun at the sun's golden glow.
As puffs of air cause a leaf to sway,
The trees chuckle, what a silly play!

Swaying high, they tell jokes so sly,
Leaves have punchlines that make spirits fly.
A lizard slides in, adds to the jest,
What's a reptile without that zest?

In this garden where humor is found,
Each leaf sings songs that are known all around.
So gather 'round tropics with smiles so wide,
Hear the palm leaves' serenade, take a ride!

A Tapestry of Shadows and Light

In the dance of shadows, we find delight,
Mischievous critiques come from left and right.
Pineapples grin from associated vines,
Sharing secrets of the sun that shines.

Fleeting guests on a whimsical route,
Pigeons have snickers – who can dispute?
With branches that wave, they giggle and twirl,
Creating a scene for the squirrels to hurl.

Oh, how the rays tease the leafy play,
Casting caricatures in a fascinating way.
Each flicker of light brings another hearty laugh,
In this canopy, both silly and daft!

So let's celebrate humor in a tapestry bright,
Within nature's arena, a canvas of light.
Where shadows hold stories, laughter takes flight,
And every green leaf feels just right!

Whispering Canopies

In the shade, where shadows stretch wide,
Squirrels chatter, their tails like a ride.
Leaves wink at the sun, teasing it so,
While ants march along, putting on a show.

Laughter bounces from tree to tree,
As coconuts plot their escape, can't you see?
A monkey swings by, with a comedic flair,
Spilling coconuts—oh, the chaos in the air!

Freckles of sunlight dance on my nose,
A gecko glides by in a comedy pose.
With every swish, the palm fronds sway,
Playing peek-a-boo in the most ridiculous way.

Lounge chairs giggle under the shade,
As if sharing secrets, a tropical parade.
The harmonica tunes from the beach sound wild,
Like nature's own orchestra, slightly beguiled.

Laughter in the Leaves

The trees are chuckling, a rustling sound,
As branches dance up, round and round.
A toucan is posing, its beak quite absurd,
While lizards are gossiping, not saying a word.

Sailboats bob like the rhythm of joy,
As seagulls squawk, what a ruckus, oh boy!
They argue with style over crumbs left behind,
A contest of wits—incredibly blind!

The shadows are laughing, teasing my feet,
With sun-soaked giggles that can't be beat.
Every flap of a wing stirs the fun,
As I watch them bicker, all under the sun.

The hammock squeaks tales of lazy delight,
While nearby, crabs dance, just out of sight.
Nature's own circus, where hilarity reigns,
In leafy arenas, where joy sustains.

Reflections on a Sunlit Path

Strolling along with a cheeky grin,
The sidewalk sparkles, asking me to spin.
As shadows leap, they mimic my stride,
Chasing each other with nothing to hide.

Birds chirp a tune, totally off-beat,
Like they're auditioning for a band, oh sweet!
I must say, it's a most curious thing,
When trees join in and start to swing.

The ocean waves laugh, tickling my toes,
A playful reminder that the fun only grows.
A crab with a pinch is a comical friend,
And he tells all the tales of a beach that won't end.

Footprints in sand make a silly parade,
Whispering jokes while the sunlight cascades.
Nature's wild gallery, a spectacle grand,
Where joy wears a crown in this sunlit land.

Hush of the Ocean Air

The ocean whispers with a playful tone,
As fish swim by, they roll and moan.
Crabs do the cha-cha on a rock near the shore,
While seashells are gossiping, wanting some more.

The waves all giggle, tickling the sand,
As seagulls plot mischief, oh isn't it grand?
A dolphin jumps high, a frolicking sprite,
Making the sunset burst with delight.

With each gentle wave comes a slapstick show,
As beach towels tumble, no place to go.
Sunhats take flight, do a twist, and then fall,
Like they're in on a joke, laughter for all.

The horizon looks on with a smirk and a grin,
As the ocean hums tunes that beckon me in.
In the hush of the evening, where smiles are sway,
Nature laughs softly, ending the day.

Secrets of a Sunlit Horizon

Under the sun with shades too bright,
A lizard danced, oh what a sight!
With flip-flops lost, we laugh and spin,
Is that a crab or my shoe? Where to begin?

In laughter's grasp, we stumble near,
A coconut fell, oh dear, oh dear!
Jokes fly high like kites above,
"Who knew we'd fall in fruit, my love?"

The sand tickles toes, a playful tease,
As gulls squawk loud, "Hey, check out these!"
With ice cream drips and sticky faces,
We race the wind in goofy paces.

With secrets shared under palm trees bold,
We mutter tales that never grow old.
As evening whispers, we just won't quit,
Funny how laughter makes moments lit.

Paradise in Motion

The hammock swings like a ride from dreams,
While mosquitoes join our sun-kissed schemes.
With drinks that clink and friends who cheer,
We toast to the day and its silly veneer!

A coconut hat, what a fine fashion!
I strut like a star, oh such passion!
But lost in a giggle, a slip, and a fall,
"Is this a dance? I'm not sure at all!"

The waves crash in with a giggling roar,
As beach balls zoom, what's in store?
We all chase shadows, a comical sight,
Running from waves that bite with delight.

In paradise, every mishap's a thrill,
With laughter that echoes, we're never still.
The sun sets low, a fabulous scene,
A vacation where fun's the routine!

Whispers of the Tropical Wind

Under the palms, our secrets flow,
With a squirrel in shades, stealing the show.
A fan of leaves, swaying with glee,
"Those are my nachos!" we shout in plea.

A parrot squawked with a cheeky grin,
"Why are you running? Come join in!"
With every giggle, a splash ignites,
"Is that my hat?" A flight of sights!

Caught in the sun, we spin around,
On this sandy stage, we dance unbound.
With nothing but laughter and funny tales,
We ride the waves, come join our trails.

The whispers swish with a tickle and tease,
As we chase memories on sides we please.
Forever trapped in this joy-filled fray,
These tropical winds will lead the way!

Dance of the Swaying Leaves

The leaves do shimmy, a leafy jive,
While we sip sodas, just trying to thrive.
A pig in the sun, what a sight it seems,
Rolling on sand like it's got great dreams!

Our shadow dances, a silly parade,
With flip-flops flapping, oh, how they swayed!
We challenge the breeze to a windy race,
"Step aside, leaves! We lead this place!"

With every laugh, a wave comes in,
We noodle like noodles, our fun's a win!
Hiccups from laughter, a sandcastle flop,
"Let's make it bigger!" the giggles won't stop.

The swaying leaves laugh along our way,
As sunset greets the end of the play.
With memories bright, in our hearts they weave,
The dance doesn't end, oh, just believe!

Evocative Dances of Nature

The leaves are shimmying, oh so spry,
They toss and twirl as if to fly.
A squirrel attempts a funky spin,
And bumps his head, good luck to win!

The flowers sway in silly pairs,
With petals waving like wild hairs.
A bee joins in with buzzing beats,
As folly fills the sunny streets.

The grass that giggles underfoot,
Makes room for ants in search of loot.
It chuckles soft with every step,
While nearby crickets dance and prep.

Nature's party rages on,
With every twist, the worries gone.
In this wild dance, all is bright,
And laughter stars the land till night.

Secrets of the Green Canopy

The vines are gossiping up high,
About the clouds that waltz and sigh.
A lizard slips, a wink in tow,
He swears he saw a butterfly show!

The ferns are fluttering like fans,
While breezy whispers trade the plans.
A parrot rehearses his best line,
But forgets it all – oh, what a sign!

Beneath the branches, shadows play,
They steal the sun and run away.
The squirrels giggle, tails like kites,
As they jump through the leafy heights.

The forest floor is a circus stage,
With critters acting in a page.
Nature's secrets, wild and free,
Bring smiles to all who come to see.

Palm Shadows and Gentle Rhythms

Shadows stretch and sway like dancers,
While sunlight flirts, giving glances.
Coconuts drop, a thud with flair,
As palm fronds wave without a care.

The beach balls bounce in silly arcs,
As seagulls join with joyous barks.
A crab scuttles in tap dance shoes,
With tiny steps, it just won't lose!

The tide plays games, it ebbs and flows,
Like a cat chasing its own tail, who knows?
With laughter echoing, the day rolls on,
Planting joy like seeds on the lawn.

A holiday feeling fills the air,
With playful pranks beyond compare.
Under the palms with humor rife,
Every moment bursts with life!

Whispered Dreams Beneath the Sun

Underneath the bright blue dome,
The critters plot to find a home.
A turtle wears a sunhat fine,
While dreaming of a giant pine.

The sunbeams tickle all in sight,
As cats embrace the pure delight.
They snooze and snore in lazy heaps,
While warmth wraps all in cozy sweeps.

A bumblebee in striped retreat,
Appears to dance with two left feet.
Next to him, a snail crawls slow,
With plans for parties down below.

With whispered dreams, the day unfolds,
In nature's laughter, joy beholds.
Life's a jest, a playful pun,
Beneath this vast and shining sun.

Tranquil Conversations with Nature

In the shade, leaves gossip low,
Chattering secrets only squirrels know.
A butterfly lands, tries to make a friend,
But the grasshopper laughs and says, 'I can't attend!'

The ants march by with a grand parade,
Debating if they should start a charade.
A twig cracks, and the whole scene shakes,
Nature's comedy, filled with mistakes.

The flowers nod, trying to keep cool,
While the sun plots pranks, feeling like a fool.
A squirrel flips, as if in a dance,
Saying, 'Watch me now, it's my take-a-chance!'

Yet in this laughter, peace finds its way,
Even the wind grins as it starts to play.
Nature's a jester, with tricks up its sleeve,
Where every petal has space to believe.

Murmurs of the Coastal Canopy

Underneath the leaves where shadows wiggle,
A crab complains, 'Why can't I wiggle?'
The cormorants chat with a touch of sass,
'Take a break, dude, stop looking like grass!'

The seaweed whispers jokes about the tide,
'Hey salty dog, come enjoy the ride!'
A pelican glides, feeling quite grand,
While jellyfish giggle, doing the stand.

Fronds flapping gently, joining the fun,
They sway to the music of a beachside run.
A turtle shows off, saying, 'Look at my shell!'
While excited sand dollars ring a weird bell.

Ocean waves play, waiting for a chat,
'Why do sea stars think they're all that?'
Laughter ripples as seabirds take flight,
Their jokes echoing, a pure delight.

Soliloquy of the Full Moon

The moon peeks out, feeling quite bold,
Saying to stars, 'I'm worth my weight in gold!'
A bit of cheese, or so they say,
But wise old owls hoot, 'No way, José!'

The crickets chirp, crafting a song,
'Hey moon, you're late, what took you so long?'
As shadows stretch in a dance of grace,
The fireflies wink, trying to keep pace.

Cold nights bring laughter, a chorus of quirks,
The raccoons debate who gets the best perks.
'You're too shiny,' mumbles a sleepy cat,
As the moon nods, 'I can't help that!'

Under this spotlight, the night's alive,
Nature's punchlines make everyone jive.
With a giggle and glow, the moon heads away,
'Catch you all later, I've got games to play!'

Gentle Tides and Floating Thoughts

Laughter flows with the splash of the sea,
'Hey octopus, did you just tease me?'
A dolphin spins, boisterous and proud,
'Your water dance is good, but I'm better wowed!'

With shells chatting tales from the deep,
Crabs shuffle around, working on their leap.
The seafoam giggles as it rolls to the shore,
Mumbling softly, 'I've done this before.'

The sand dunes chuckle, storing secrets untold,
While driftwood cackles, aging and old.
A seagull squawks jokes that sparks a cheer,
As waves play tag, nothing to fear.

Floating thoughts drift beneath and around,
As shells crack up laughing, their humor profound.
The tides bring joy, a comic delight,
Where every splash enlivens the night.

Whispers of the Tropical Wind

In the shade where laughter hides,
The leaves play tag as the sunlight glides.
Coconuts take bets on who'll drop first,
While parrots gossip, their voices burst.

A lizard does a wiggly dance,
While ants form lines, as if in a trance.
They march to beats of nature's drum,
As monkeys giggle and call out, "Come!"

Hammocks swing with a gentle sway,
As someone snores a loud 'olé!'
But what's that ruckus on the ground?
A crab out strutting, so proud, so round!

From the cliff, the view's a treat,
Both foolish and lovely, oh, what a feat!
Palm fronds wave, as if they know,
The silly secrets of the show.

Dance of the Dappled Leaves

Leaves do the cha-cha in a breezy show,
With the raindrops joining in to flow.
Sunlight peeks from clouds above,
Tickling trees with a golden shove.

Squirrels play catch with acorns nearby,
While a pigeon tries to take off and fly.
But it trips and flops, then gives a squawk,
Waddling off like an awkward rock!

The shadows flicker, a playful sight,
As the wind whispers jokes, what a delight!
A toucan laughs, its beak so wide,
Sharing puns from the sky, unqualified!

Dance, little leaves, with all your grace,
As we chuckle at nature's funny face.
With each rustle, we join in the fun,
Under the sun, our laughter's never done!

Serenade in the Canopy

Up high where the shadows flirt and sway,
A sloth hums tunes to start the day.
While birds in the branches chirp their song,
The chorus gets louder, can't be wrong!

A parrot takes the stage with flair,
Dancing and twirling, without a care.
It forgets the words and just goes 'squawk!',
Leaving the crowd in stitches to gawk!

A monkey swings in, steals the show,
Napping props, 'what a pro!'
The sunbeams spotlight their playful spree,
As palm leaves clap in harmony.

Under this canopy, fun takes a stand,
With laughter echoing across the land.
So join the serenade without delay,
Nature's rhythm makes for a wild ballet!

Secrets Carried by the Trade Winds

The winds are chattering, oh so sly,
Spreading secrets as they flutter by.
A crab knitting gossip into a shell,
While monkeys laugh, they know it well.

Whispers about coconuts in a race,
Which one will roll with the fastest grace?
While palm trees giggle, they sway and bend,
As if to say, 'Oh, this will never end!'

A gecko's busy painting its toes,
While a lazy dog snoozes, a real doze.
They chat about fish and their wild escapades,
And the tales of the rain come out as parades.

With every gust, the laughter flows,
In this tropical realm, anything goes.
Come hear the tales the sweet winds bring,
In the jungle's embrace, let your heart sing!

Poetry of the Swaying Fronds

The leaves are dancing, what a show,
A palm tree party, oh so slow.
One frond winks at another with flair,
Is it a dance, or just hot air?

The coconuts giggle when they sway,
They whisper secrets in a playful way.
A crow takes flight, almost missteps,
While the sunbeams laugh, in tiny reps.

Who knew a leaf could tickle the sky?
With every gust, it seems to fly!
Are those dance moves or just a tease?
One thing's for sure, they sure aim to please!

So here's to the palms, let's raise a cheer,
For the laughter and fun, they bring all year.
Stick around folks, you won't want to leave,
For nature's sandbox, it's hard to believe!

Gentle Pulses of the Tropic

In the shade, a soft rustle we hear,
Palms exchanging gossip, never fear!
One leaf said, 'I've got it made,'
While another sways, feeling dismayed.

The sun pokes fun at their silly games,
As shadows stretch out and call them names.
'Who tipped the breeze?', the old trunk sighs,
While the sunbeams giggle, ducking for highs.

Even the sand seems to join this spat,
As footprints dance, and then fall flat.
A crab walks by, nudging with pride,
'Come on, buddies, let's take a ride!'

And oh, how they sway, in this soft light,
Their laughter carries into the night.
Here's to the moments they happily mold,
In the whispers of palms, adventures unfold!

A Serenade of Natural Wonders

The leaves shake hands with the passing air,
Whistling tunes, like they just don't care.
A squirrel joins in, with a cheeky smile,
He pirouettes, and stays a while.

'Did you see that move?', a leaf does boast,
While another flutters like a friendly ghost.
Coconuts chuckle, rolling their eyes,
At the grand show that nature supplies.

The sun throws confetti from the sky,
While shadows breathe, and then, they sigh.
'What's next, my friend?' a twig boldly asks,
'Let's plan a trip, maybe wear some masks!'

So here they gather, to dream and to play,
In the golden rays, they spend the day.
With laughter echoing, a joyous salute,
To the symphony where fun can't be moot!

Twilight Enchantment Beneath the Leaves

As the sun dips low, the fun begins,
Fronds shake hands, sharing silly spins.
'Who's afraid of the dark?' one leaf muses,
While shadows giggle, losing their excuses.

A gentle swirl, the night unfolds,
Whispers of mischief, stories told.
Coconuts strut, feeling quite grand,
While crickets chirp, joining the band.

The moon looks down, a cheeky grin,
Watching the leaves as their dance starts to spin.
A firefly twirls, steals the spotlight bright,
Nature's spectacle, a true delight!

So beneath the leaves, let laughter resound,
For when twilight sings, joy knows no bound.
Join in the fun, don't let it pass,
In the heart of the night, we're free at last!

Caress of the Coastal Shadows

The shadows stretch as the sun retreats,
Silly crabs play tag on sandy seats.
With a flip and a flop, they scurry fast,
Waving their claws, but they sure won't last.

A parrot squawks, doing quite a dance,
Stealing the spotlight, taking a chance.
He fluffs his feathers like he's in charge,
While squirrels gossip, sounding quite large.

The waves giggle softly, tickling the shore,
As shells whisper secrets, "Who could want more?"
A flip flop flies, almost hits a whale,
Who laughs out loud, "Oh, tell me a tale!"

Shrimp in a cocktail, wearing a hat,
Ponder their lives, and where they are at.
With a wink and a wiggle, they dance in the sun,
Claiming the day, "Oh boy, this is fun!"

Fragrant Journeys Beneath the Skies

A mango drops, what a juicy surprise,
While seagulls plot with mischievous eyes.
They snatch and they swoop, what a noisy crew,
"Who knew a snack could taste so good too?"

Coconut hats float down from the trees,
As monkeys hang out, they do just as they please.
With each little swing, their laughter erupts,
Slinging their snacks at friends who get plucked!

Fragrant blooms giggle, tickled by air,
Inviting a lizard to trade quite a stare.
"A lizard in bloom, is he quite the prize?"
"Or just a leaf that forgot how to rise?"

The sun starts to set, painting skies with delight,
While ants throw a party, oh, what a sight!
They dance in a line, making quite the parade,
"Who needs a disco? We've already made!"

Fluttering Paradise

Butterflies chatter, with wigs full of flair,
"Is this the best garden? Oh, I do declare!"
They strut with their colors, more vivid than paint,
"Do we make flowers blush? Oh, one can't faint!"

A curious hedgehog rolls in the grass,
Wishing to join in, hoping he'll pass.
"Can I borrow some wings? Just for a flight!"
"Sorry, dear friend, you'll stick out in sight!"

Bumblebees bustle, conducting their choir,
Harmonizing softly, fueling the fire.
"With honey, we flourish, but where's the fun?"
"Let's paint this dull world, till the day is done!"

A tortoise shimmies, rare sight to behold,
Betting with friends he'll finally be bold.
"Step right up, folks, it's a race not to miss!"
But off in the distance, here comes the bliss!"

A Soft Touch of Nature

Waves chuckle softly, tickling the coast,
While fish salute, they seem to boast.
"Did you see that jump? It was quite a show!"
"Just wait till I flip; I'll steal the whole floe!"

With sandy toes, a toddler yells loud,
Taking a tumble, oh, what a proud crowd!
"Did you see that splat? What a glorious fall!"
The gulls throw their heads back, cackling for all!

Palm trees are high-fiving, swaying in cheer,
Gossiping stories from the bright, warm sphere.
"Grab your sun hats; the party's outside!"
As a coconut drops like a bumpy joyride!

Insects host dances, their rhythm so sweet,
With tiny ball gowns and very small feet.
They twirl 'round the daisies, making a fuss,
"Who needs a thrill? Nature's fun is a must!"

Sunset Over the Palm Grove

The sun wore a hat, a bright orange glow,
While coconut crabs danced, putting on quite a show.
A parrot squawked jokes, perched high on a tree,
Laughter echoed around, so wild and free.

A hammock swung low, caught in the game,
As a squirrel ran past, chasing a flame.
The sky turned to candy, purple and pink,
While fish in the pond shared secrets, I think.

Lizards in shades, sunbathing with flair,
Gossiping loudly, their tales to compare.
With each passing cloud, their drama unfolds,
The gossiping lizards, the funniest told.

The day tumbled down, like a clumsy old friend,
As laughter and laughter seemed never to end.
Under palm tree umbrellas, we soaked in the sights,
With giggles and grins, we embraced the warm nights.

Flickering Light Through the Lush

At twilight, we gathered, lanterns aglow,
Chasing shadows that danced, putting on quite a show.
With beetles as dancers, they twirled in a line,
And a frog jumped in rhythm, croaking out time.

A cat in a palm tree, a purr of delight,
Swatting at moths in the flickering light.
'Catch me if you can!' the bold fireflies chimed,
As giggles erupted, we all felt so primed.

Funny faces were drawn, our shadows took flight,
As palm fronds swayed softly, our spirits felt light.
Under starlit giggles, we played hide and seek,
In this whirlwind of joy, we were happily meek.

With laughter and whispers, secrets were spun,
The night painted pictures of frolic and fun.
Amongst dew-drenched leaves, we jostled and spun,
As lights flickered on, the magic begun.

Harmony in the Wind's Embrace

The whispers were loud, like a chatty young kid,
As the palms shared secrets, their laughter well hid.
A monkey on a branch, with a banana to munch,
Winked at me slyly, said, 'Join in for lunch!'

The wind played piano, oh such a sweet song,
While squirrels spun tales that just went on too long.
A parakeet squawked, on its high-flying quest,
"Life's a funny game, just put on your best!"

The sun dipped and chuckled, painting the skies,
While crickets were sentries, protecting the pies.
Under giggly shadows, we all played our parts,
In a symphony woven with whimsical hearts.

So let's toast to the winds, juggling giggles galore,
With palms as our witnesses, we shout out for more.
In the nighttime's embrace, where sweet laughter thrums,
We're all just big kids, embracing the fun.

The Dance of Sunlit Shadows

In the midday sun, shadows leapt on the bay,
As the palms did a jig, in a carefree display.
A crab with a hat, tipped it ever so low,
While dancing with glee, said, "Come join the show!"

By the water's edge, a turtle wore shades,
Swaying to the rhythm, enjoying the glades.
"Who needs to hurry?" it called with a cheer,
"When life is so fun, hold your laughter near!"

The sun giggled brightly, playing peek-a-boo,
As shadows stretched long, weaving stories anew.
And in this bright dance, we rolled on the grass,
With every good joke, we found it would last.

So let's twirl with the shadows, each laugh a delight,
In this sunlit embrace, everything feels right.
With palms as our partners, we'd spin 'til we drop,
In the dance of pure joy, we just can't stop.

Enchantment Amidst the Green

In the jungle gym of trees,
Monkeys play and swing with glee,
Kites get tangled, high in fun,
Nature's playground, never done.

Lizards laugh, they do the twist,
Avoiding paws—oh, the great mist!
A parrot squawks a funny jest,
While squirrels prepare for their best quest.

Shadows dance, creating art,
As giggles bounce from heart to heart,
The sun dips low, a golden beam,
In the green, we chase our dream.

Come find the charm where smiles are shared,
In this realm, no one is scared,
With every chuckle, spirits rise,
Enchantment gleams in laughing eyes.

Harbor of Gentle Whispers

Swaying leaves share secrets sweet,
As crickets hum a silly beat,
The sunbeams wink, the shadows tease,
The air is filled with tickling breeze.

Frogs in tuxedos jump for joy,
While dancing ants parade a toy,
The flowers nod their colorful heads,
Joining in on nature's spreads.

With giggles rising from below,
The winds play tag, a playful show,
Here we frolic, laugh, and cheer,
In this safe port, we shed our fear.

So let the whispers swirl and glide,
As laughter fills the countryside,
In this fun-filled leafy place,
We find our joy, and we embrace.

Heartbeats in the Canopy's Shade

Underneath the leafy veil,
Laughter echoes, tell a tale,
Of a sloth taking a quick nap,
Then suddenly, a jump and flap!

A squirrel's stash of nuts is lost,
He searches high—oh, what a cost!
The sun peeks through with cheeky mirth,
As joy erupts on nature's turf.

Leaves rustle like a giggling crew,
With butterflies that joke and flew,
In shadows where the wild things roam,
We find our laughter finds a home.

So here in nature's wild embrace,
With every chuckle, we find grace,
In canopy's shade, let joy cascade,
Where heartbeats dance, and memories made.

Nature's Artistic Caress

With strokes of green and dashes bright,
Nature paints a scene so light,
Where daisies giggle, daisies dance,
Waiting for a flutter's chance.

The wind gets playful, pushing leaves,
It sneaks a tickle, oh, who believes?
A wild boar rolls in the mud,
Creating art with every thud.

Pine cones tumble, land with a plop,
Creating chaos, it won't stop,
A rabbit hops and plays the fool,
Bouncing through the leafy school.

So join the laughter, twirl and swing,
In this artful play, we sing,
With nature's charm, we'll not suppress,
The joy we find in this caress.

Rustling Pages of the Earth

Leaves dance and giggle, a silly show,
Swaying like they know where to go.
A bug with a bowtie joins the delight,
Fumbling his way into the night.

Flip-flops slap on the sandy floor,
As laughter echoes, wanting more.
The sun hides, peeking too shy to play,
As the earth spins tales of yesterday.

A squirrel in shades steals the scene,
Practicing moves like a dancing machine.
While grasshoppers chirp their silly tune,
Together they twirl 'neath the cheeky moon.

With each rustle, the planet brews,
A comedy of nature, just for a few.
So close your eyes and hear the mirth,
In the rustling pages of our dear Earth.

Palms in the Twilight Glow

Tall figures swaying with a wink,
As shadows stretch, they start to blink.
A tropical whisper tells a jest,
Every palm tree is ready for rest.

Sunset's laugh spills colors bright,
While coconuts fall with a gentle slight.
One rolls away, chasing a dream,
"I swear I was here!" it protests with a scream.

Laughter from crickets fills the air,
As fireflies flash like they don't care.
A turtle in a tie stumbles nearby,
"Is this the dance floor? Oh my, oh my!"

While the stars twinkle, the palms still sway,
In the twilight glow, they dance and play.
Fruits drop down, plop, with a bounce,
"Oh no, not again!" says the coconut ounce.

Gentle Currents of Paradise

Waves giggle softly, tickling the shore,
While seagulls squawk, "Give us more!"
A crab in a flip-flop strutted proud,
Claiming the sand in a proud little crowd.

The sun wears shades, looking sublime,
While fish crack jokes, as if on time.
A dolphin splashes, "Did you see that?
I'm the fastest! Just look at this splat!"

Tropical drinks come with tiny umbrellas,
Cheeky little sippers, those daring fellas.
"A drink in each fin! Let's all take a dip!"
This paradise party brings smiles and a sip.

From the gentle sways of leafy green,
A party unfolds, a hilarious scene.
In currents of wonder, all laughter springs,
As nature unravels its funny little things.

Whirling Whispers of Serenity

In the stillness, whispers prance,
Like shy ballerinas lost in a trance.
Clouds play tag, fluffed and serene,
While sunset giggles at the lovely scene.

A tortoise in sneakers ties them tight,
Saying, "I'm fast! Just you wait 'til night!"
The wind roars back, "Oh really, dear?
Don't trip on your laces, or we may cheer!"

Each fluttering leaf adds to the jest,
Swirling around like they're on a quest.
A gust sneezes; papers go flying,
"Guess I'm the wind!" the branches are trying.

As dusk unfolds its soft, warm beds,
Nature's whispers fill our heads.
In serenity's dance, hilarity thrives,
The world spins laughter, as joy arrives.

Ocean's Breath Among the Trees

In the shade where coconuts sway,
A crab claims his throne, come what may.
He waves his claws, a royal decree,
"Stay off my lunch, or you'll pay a fee!"

A parrot squawks, with style and flair,
"Watch my moves, if you dare compare!"
Her dance makes the toucan roll its eyes,
"You're just a rainbow with legs that size!"

Along comes a monkey, swinging with glee,
"Hey there, folks, come climb with me!"
He trips on a vine, oh what a sight,
"Guess I'll stick to the ground; this feels just right!"

As the sun sets low, the fun won't cease,
These critters will party, they've got the keys.
To laughter and joy, we'll sing all night,
In the palms where the silly creatures take flight!

Tranquil Echoes of Palms

Among the leaves, a stillness reigns,
Yet Billy the squirrel has no such chains.
He's practicing flips, in the sun's warm glow,
"Watch and learn, folks, I'm the star of the show!"

A lizard observes, with a smug little grin,
"What're you doing, Billy? You're not even thin!"
"You're just jealous, I can leap and spin,
But do you just sit there, you lazy skin?"

A turtle stirs, at a slow, charming pace,
"You'll tire yourself out in this crazy race!"
"Not if I catch some z's on this branch,
Because life is too short for a serious stance!"

At dusk the trees hum their evening tune,
While laughter spills out, under the moon.
In the breezy palms, where humor resides,
The antics of nature can't be denied!

Fluttering Leaves' Tale

Leaves whisper secrets in a playful breeze,
As Sammy the sloth hangs from a tree with ease.
"I'm just hanging out, life's not a race,
Why rush around when you can embrace?"

A butterfly flutters, with style on display,
"Sammy, dear friend, let's dance, come what may!"
He yawns widely, and then shakes his head,
"I'd rather just nap, and dream instead!"

The sunbeams chuckle, as shadows parade,
While lizards play tag in a sun-soaked glade.
"I'm the champion!" yells a gecko so spry,
While the others just smile with a knowing sigh.

In this leafy kingdom, laughter takes flight,
Every creature knows where the fun feels right.
They bask in the joy, natural and free,
In a world where even sloths can feel glee!

The Quiet Symphony of Nature

In the cool of the shade, where the sunlight beams,
Frogs croak their warnings, igniting the dreams.
"Hop on over, join our silly choir,
Sing the praises of mud and the things we require!"

Crickets chime in, with their fiddles in tow,
"Let's make this a concert, let everybody know!"
A snail takes the stage, with slow-motion flair,
"Could someone give me a ride? I'm a bit unaware!"

The trees sway gently to the humor-filled tunes,
As a raccoon joins in, tossing ripe prunes.
"Let's host a buffet, with a feast to enjoy!
And make the ants work for the joy of the ploy!"

As twilight descends, the laughter rings clear,
In the symphony of nature, there's nothing to fear.
For in every rustle and giggle we find,
That the spirit of fun is humankind's bind!

www.ingramcontent.com/pod-product-compliance
Lightning Source LLC
Chambersburg PA
CBHW072124070526
44585CB00016B/1544